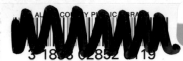 

HAKEEM
OLAJUWON

(Photo on front cover.)

Hakeem Olajuwon (34) fights for a rebound with Scottie Pippen (33) of the Chicago Bulls.

(Photo on previous pages.)

Olajuwon is named the NBA's Most Valuable Player in 1994.

Photography supplied by Wide World Photos Inc.

Library of Congress Cataloging-in-Publication Data
Rambeck, Richard.
Hakeem Olajuwon / Richard Rambeck.
p. cm.
Summary: Relates the basketball career of the
Nigerian-born star center of the Houston Rockets who
won his first championship after eleven seasons in
the National Basketball Association.
ISBN 1-56766-200-5 (lib. Bdg.)
1. Olajuwon, Hakeem. 1963- —Juvenile literature.
2. Basketball players—United States—Biography—
Juvenile literature. [1. Olajuwon, Hakeem, 1963-.
2. Basketball players. 3. Blacks-Nigeria—Biography.]
I. Title
GV884.043R35 1995   95-5625
796.323'092— dc20   CIP
[B]   AC

HAKEEM
OLAJUWON

BY RICHARD RAMBECK

As the clock ticked down to zero, the ball was where it belonged. It was in the big hands of Hakeem Olajuwon, the star center of the Houston Rockets. He cradled the ball as the seventh and final game of the 1994 National Basketball Association finals ended. Olajuwon's Rockets won the seventh game 90–84 over the New York Knicks. Houston was the NBA champion, and Olajuwon finally had the league title he had spent 11 years chasing.

Until 1994, Olajuwon had done everything an NBA basketball player could do — except win a championship. "Not only is he the best big man in the game, he's the best player," said Seattle coach George Karl. Shaquille O'Neal, a big star himself, agreed with Karl. "I have no problem with Hakeem being called the best player in the game," said O'Neal, the center for the Orlando Magic. "He's got great moves and a great attitude."

And finally, Hakeem Olajuwon had a championship. For a while, it looked as if he would never win one. In college at the University of Houston, his team reached the NCAA championship game twice, but lost both times. In 1983, Houston was upset by North Carolina State in the NCAA finals. In 1984, Olajuwon outplayed Georgetown center

Patrick Ewing in the finals. Olajuwon had 15 points to Ewing's 10, but Houston still lost to Georgetown 84–75.

Olajuwon, who was born in Nigeria, was the first player picked in the 1984 NBA draft. He was taken even ahead of Michael Jordan, who was drafted third by the Chicago Bulls. The seven-foot-tall Olajuwon helped turn the Houston Rockets from a bad team into a good one. In Olajuwon's second season, 1985–86, the Rockets made it all the way to the NBA finals against the Boston Celtics, but Boston took the title by winning four out of six games.

"After losing in the finals in 1986, I said, 'Next time I go, we win.' And I meant it," Olajuwon said. "I figured I'd get there three or four more times. I was so young." It took the Rockets a long time to get back to the finals, but in the meantime, Olajuwon just got better and better. He led the NBA in rebounding in the 1988–89 and 1989–90 seasons. He was the league's top shot blocker in 1989–90 and 1990–91.

Olajuwon was also one of the leading scorers in the NBA. "Offensively, he can't be stopped," said Houston coach Rudy Tomjanovich. "Defensively, people are afraid to drive to the basket. He's a

**Olajuwon
dunks one at
Madison
Square
Garden.**

monster shot blocker." Olajuwon wanted to score, but he took more pride in his defense. When players tried to drive to the basket against Houston, he wanted them to know he was around. "I try to block everything," he said.

While Olajuwon was becoming one of the top players in the game, the Rockets were slipping in the standings. They didn't even make the playoffs after the 1991–92 season. Some fans thought the Rockets should trade Olajuwon. Some felt he wasn't as good as he had once been. "If people thought of me as going down, it was only because the team had gone down," he said. The team and

Olajuwon would soon be going back up.

The Rockets posted a 55–27 record in the 1992–93 season. They won the NBA's Midwest Division and had the fourth best record in the league. Olajuwon was the NBA's top shot blocker, with more than four a game. He was also the league's fourth highest scorer (21.1 points a game) and fourth best rebounder (13.0 a game). Olajuwon was also named to the NBA's all-league team. Still, Houston lost to Seattle in the second round of the playoffs.

When the 1993–94 season began, it was as if everyone had forgotten about Olajuwon and the Rockets. Michael

Olajuwon celebrates with teammate Vernon Maxwell during a playoff game.

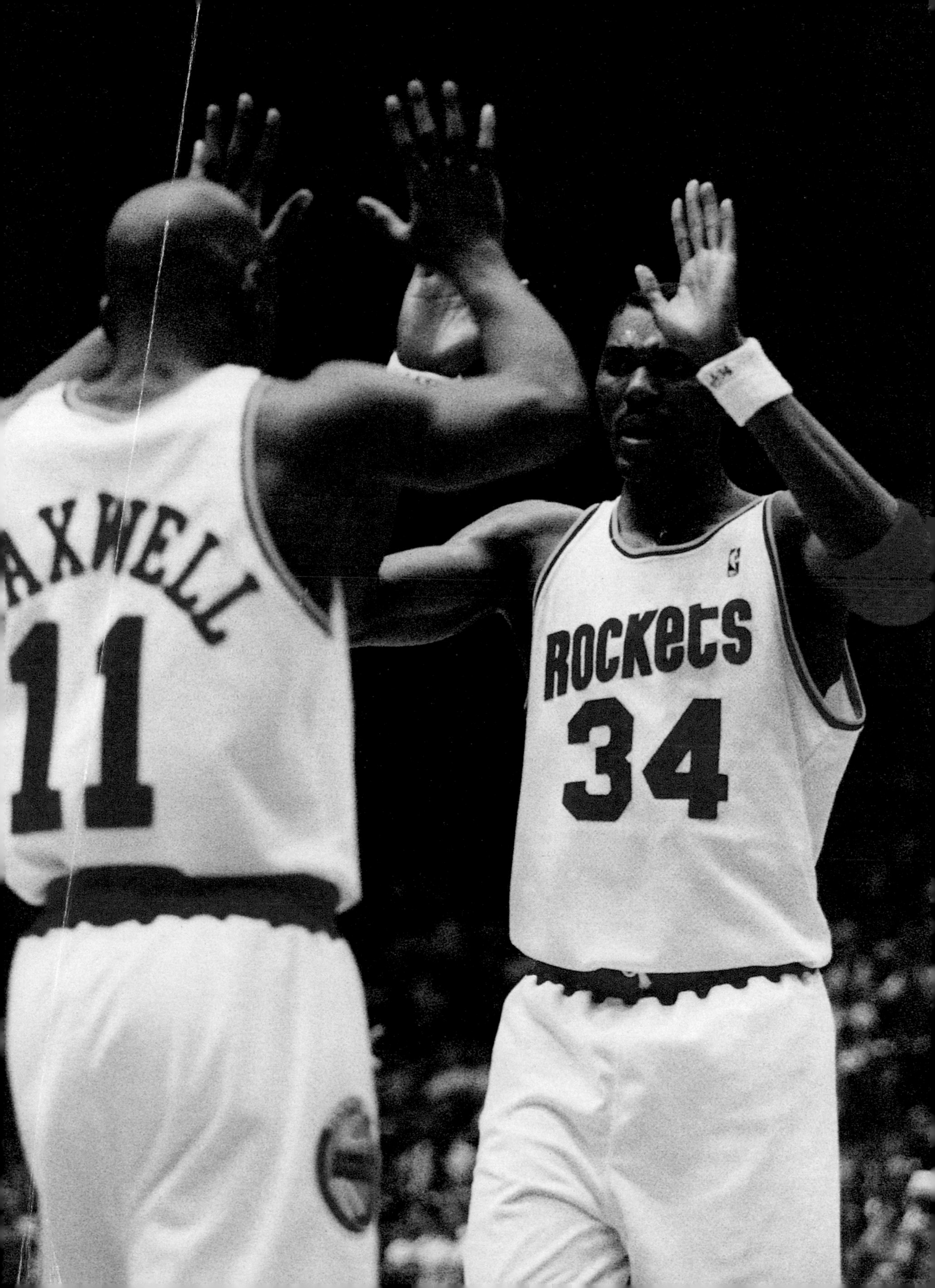
AXWELL
11
ROCKETS
34

Jordan had retired after leading Chicago to three straight championships. The experts said New York, Phoenix, and Seattle had the best chance to win the 1993–94 title. And Houston? The Rockets had won their first 15 games of the season. Olajuwon wound up the season as the league's fourth highest scorer and third best rebounder.

Houston won the Midwest Division again. But when the playoffs started, New York, Phoenix, and Seattle were still the teams favored to win the title. Seattle, however, was upset by Denver in the first round of the playoffs. Then Houston beat Phoenix in the second round. The Rockets were closer to the league finals than they had been since 1986. Houston faced the Utah Jazz for the Western Conference championship, and the Rockets proved to be Utah's worst nightmare.

Felton Spencer was one of the Utah centers who tried to guard Olajuwon. "Sometimes I get dizzy if I try to look at how he moves his feet on the floor," Spencer said. "It was funny. Olajuwon had 29 points in one game, and everybody is telling me, 'You did a great job of stopping him.'" Utah couldn't stop Olajuwon and the Rockets. Houston won the series four games to one. The Rockets were in the

NBA finals again, and this time, they wouldn't lose.

The New York Knicks, however, won three of the first five games of the series. The Rockets went home for the final two games knowing they had to win both to take the title. Led by Olajuwon's rebounding and defense, the Rockets won games six and seven. Olajuwon was named Most Valuable Player of the series. He was also MVP of the league and Defensive Player of the Year. Finally, after 11 seasons in the NBA, Hakeem Olajuwon had won his first championship.